GOD CAN NOT BE TRUSTED

GOD CAN NOT BE TRUSTED

LIFECHANGE BOOKS

TONY EVANS

Multnomah® Publishers *Sisters, Oregon*

GOD CAN NOT BE TRUSTED (AND FIVE OTHER LIES OF SATAN)
published by Multnomah Publishers, Inc.

© 2005 by Tony Evans
International Standard Book Number: 1-59052-417-9

Cover Kirk DouPonce, DogEaredDesign.com
Cover image by John Silver

Unless otherwise indicated, Scripture quotations are from:
The Holy Bible, English Standard Version (ESV) © 2001 by Crossway Bibles,
a division of Good News Publishers. Used by permission. All rights reserved.
Other Scripture quotations are from:
New American Standard Bible® (NASB) © 1960, 1977, 1995
by the Lockman Foundation. Used by permission.
The Holy Bible, New International Version (NIV) © 1973, 1984 by International Bible
Society, used by permission of Zondervan Publishing House

Multnomah is a trademark of Multnomah Publishers, Inc.,
and is registered in the U.S. Patent and Trademark Office.
The colophon is a trademark of Multnomah Publishers, Inc.

Printed in the United States of America

For information:
MULTNOMAH PUBLISHERS, INC. • 601 N. LARCH ST. • SISTERS, OR 97759

Library of Congress Cataloging-in-Publication Data
Evans, Anthony T.
  God can not be trusted (and five other lies of Satan) / Tony Evans.
    p. cm.
  ISBN 1-59052-417-9
  1. Providence and government of God. 2. Trust in God. 3. Devil. I. Title:
God cannot be trusted (and five other lies of Satan). II. Title.
  BT96.3.E93 2005
  231.7--dc22

                          2005011927

05 06 07 08 09 10—10 9 8 7 6 5 4 3 2 1 0

CONTENTS

INTRODUCTION

THE FATHER OF LIES

Have you ever heard it said of someone who wasn't the most honest person in the world that "he wouldn't know the truth if it bit him"?

Today, it's not considered politically correct to call someone a liar, even if everyone can see that the person has a problem telling the truth. But when Jesus walked the earth, He didn't hesitate for a second to refer to His number one enemy using that very word:

> "He was a murderer from the beginning, and has nothing to do with the truth, because there is no truth in him. When he lies, he speaks out of his

own character, for he is a liar and the father of
lies."

JOHN 8:44

That murderer Jesus referred to, not just as a liar, but
as "the father of lies," is Satan. When it comes to lying,
deceiving, and twisting the truth, the devil is truly in a
class all his own. He's a liar by his very nature, and his
entire motivation—his reason for being—is to lie and
deceive.

Part of what makes the devil such an effective liar—I'd
say the best who ever lived—is that he's extremely smart.
He knows how to manipulate and work through this
world's systems. He also knows our strengths, our weaknesses, and the things we "like" when it comes to sin. And
after doing these things for thousands and thousands of
years, he's perfected them.

In the Bible, we first read of Satan's lying ways in the
third chapter of the book of Genesis. The devil appears to
Eve as a snake in the Garden of Eden and begins spewing
his deceptions in an effort to get her to do the one thing
God had told her and Adam not to do, namely, eat the fruit
from the tree of the knowledge of good and evil.

Satan lied, Eve believed him, and the world was

thrown into chaos. But that doesn't mean the devil is done lying. Not by a long shot!

Adam and Eve lived in a perfect environment where there was no sin or death. Yet Satan was right there, throwing around his deceptions and lies. Now if the devil came at these folks who knew nothing of sin or evil, what do you think he wants to do to you and me, people who are exposed to all kinds of evil every day of our lives?

We simply don't have the option of just ignoring Satan or his lies. To do that would be to give him a huge head start in his deception. No, the devil's lies must be confronted, refuted, and defeated once and for all. But how do we do that?

This may surprise you, but you can't beat the devil. He's far too powerful, intelligent, and crafty for even the most gifted among us. We can't overcome the devil through positive thinking, through gritting our teeth and working harder, or through making the most sincere resolution to "do better."

If we go face-to-face with the devil using those kinds of personal strengths, it's "game over" before we even start.

So far, this seems like a pretty hopeless situation, doesn't it? It sounds like no matter what we do, the devil's going to win. But it's far from hopeless, because God has given us the one weapon that will defeat Satan and his lies every time: *the truth*.

The devil can handle anything we throw at him in our own strength, but the one thing he absolutely *can't* handle is the truth, and especially the truth of Jesus Christ as it's recorded in the Bible.

The Bible isn't just a book full of nice stories and good life principles. The Bible is truth—God's truth. It's eternal, complete, and all-powerful truth that easily takes the devil's lies and puts them in their place. When that happens, we have the abundant, victorious life God has promised us.

This little book you're holding right now lists the six biggest lies of Satan and, more importantly, how the truth of the Word of God overwhelmingly and eternally counteracts and refutes each of those lies.

As you read on, you may recognize times in your life when Satan has sent one of his whoppers your way. It is my hope that you won't just recognize the lies you've been told, but that you'll be empowered to do something about them.

LIE #1

SATAN DOES NOT EXIST

In the short story "The Generous Gambler" by nineteenth-century poet Charles Baudelaire, a preacher says, "My dear brethren, do not ever forget...that the loveliest trick of the Devil is to persuade you that he does not exist."

Satan's first and probably most important lie is that he's nothing more than a fable. The devil does everything he can to convince us that he's not real or that if he is real, his existence shouldn't matter to us because he can't do anything to us.

Why do you think a character of such pride and arrogance wants us to believe either that he's a myth or that he doesn't spend his time thinking of ways to harass us? Because he knows that if an enemy isn't perceived as real or as a threat, then it is easier for that enemy to attack and do damage.

But the Bible has some very direct warnings about Satan and what he has the power to do. Over and over, the Scriptures tell us there is a real devil and that he works tirelessly to harass humanity in general and the people of God in particular, hoping to either keep us from Christ or to make us ineffective for the kingdom of God.

As the Word of God tells us, the devil didn't wait long before he began to do his evil business with us humans.

A REAL SNAKE IN THE GRASS

As I said earlier, Satan first made his appearance in human history way back in the Garden of Eden. God had finished His creation and everything was perfect. There was no sin, no fear, and no death. Adam and Eve were so comfortable with themselves and with their God that they walked around this indescribably beautiful garden completely naked but felt no shame or embarrassment (Genesis 2:25).

Enter Satan to begin his temptation of humankind: "Now the serpent was more crafty than any other beast of the field that the LORD God had made. He said to the woman, 'Did God actually say...?'" (Genesis 3:1).

Not only do we have a crafty snake, but we have a crafty snake who can talk in Eve's own language. But what's really startling about this scene is that the woman seems unfazed by what she's seeing and hearing.

The devil had achieved his objective of sneaking up on Eve without her knowing that it was actually the tempter in snake's clothing.

As we read of the serpent tempting Eve, we suspect that it's actually the devil taking the form of a snake. And later on in Scripture, we see with certainty who the serpent really was. The passage that spells it out for us is in the book of Revelation: "And the great dragon was thrown down, *that ancient serpent*, who is called the devil and Satan, the deceiver of the whole world—he was thrown down to the earth, and his angels were thrown down with him" (Revelation 12:9, italics mine). Later in Revelation we read, "And he seized the dragon, *that ancient serpent*, who is the devil and Satan, and bound him for a thousand years" (Revelation 20:2, italics mine).

But how did the devil get here in the first place? The Bible gives us the story.

HOW THE DEVIL GOT HIS START

Before God created humans, He created angels, the chief among them being one named Lucifer. The name "Lucifer" literally means the "shining one," and he was certainly that. Ezekiel 28:13–14 describes him as a magnificent created being who was called "an anointed cherub." This means that God had a special and blessed purpose for creating Lucifer.

Originally, Lucifer's reason for being was to lead all the other angels in the worship of God, and for a while everything went according to God's plan. But one day Lucifer looked at himself in the mirror, saw his own spectacular beauty, and began to be filled with pride. His pride was so great that he wanted what God says no created being will ever have: equality with God Himself.

Lucifer's pride and arrogance led him to rebel against God, a scene recorded in Isaiah 14, where Lucifer says five times, "I will." The devil was a proud, willful angel who wanted power and position far above any created being, equal in fact to that of God Himself.

Lucifer attempted a celestial coup d'état against God's eternal rule, leading a third of the millions of angels in rebellion. Of course, simple logic tells us that it's impossible to rebel successfully against God who knows all, even the thoughts of those He has created. Lucifer's plan was quickly uncovered, and he was declared guilty of cosmic treason and thrown, along with the angels who had joined him in rebellion, out of heaven to the earth, where to this day he awaits his eternal punishment.

When God placed Adam and Eve in the Garden of Eden, Creation itself was perfect. But already wandering around the earth was Satan, who was eager to do all he could to continue his rebellion against the Creator.

Now, why would God allow a perfect Creation to be corrupted by the presence of evil? Why was Satan allowed to tempt Eve? Why didn't God just step in and crush the devil and keep His Creation in its perfect state?

The answer lies in something we can't fully understand: the nature of God's love for all of us.

LOVE MEANS ALLOWING FOR CHOICES

When God created humankind, He made us the crown jewel of His creation. God made humans "in his own image" (Genesis 1:27). He wanted us to be lower than Him but also very much like Him in that we had a free will and the capacity to respond to Him in love and obedience. God didn't want millions of little robots who had no choice but to obey Him; He wanted beings who could *choose* to respond in obedience.

God never forced anyone to be obedient to Him. Yes, He blesses those who obey and He punishes those who disobey, but He wants more than anything for us to *choose* to obey Him. That was the choice Adam and Eve faced in the Garden.

It's also the choice we face today. And we need to know that Satan is still prowling around looking for ways to throw us off balance and to distract us from doing what we need to do so that we can be what God wants us to be.

CONSTANTLY ON THE PROWL

Genesis 3:1 tells us that the devil in snake's clothing was "more crafty than any other beast of the field." Another word we can use to describe the devil is *cunning*. Still another word we can use is *shrewd*. We have a spiritual enemy who is brilliant and who has all the tricks of the trade when it comes to deceiving, lying, and trying to trip us up. But there's even more to Satan's craftiness than that.

I recently did a little research on snakes, and one thing I found about them reminded me of something the Bible tells us about Satan. I found out that snakes don't blink because they don't have eyelids; snakes' eyes are always open. That means that snakes can always see and are always on the prowl looking for prey.

That is so much like our spiritual enemy, who the Bible tells us is on the lookout 24/7, searching for ways to trip us up and swallow us up. The apostle Peter warned his readers about Satan's prowling ways: "Be sober-minded; be watchful. Your adversary the devil prowls around like a roaring lion, seeking someone to devour" (1 Peter 5:8).

Satan also bears a resemblance to a snake in that he's very quiet when he needs to be. Anyone who's ever encountered a snake in the wild will tell you that you often don't see them until you're right on top of them. That's because they stay very still while they wait for some unfortunate critter to happen by and become their dinner.

We can't expect to receive a warning as Satan prepares to pull something on us. His attacks aren't usually big, spectacular events we see coming. Satan is crafty, and oftentimes he just waits quietly for his opportunity to strike a blow against us.

But there's something else we need to know about the devil. As crafty and smart as he is, he knows how to dress himself up in a way that keeps our fears and suspicions at bay.

DRESSED TO KILL

I've always been a fan of science fiction. I especially love those old movies and television shows that feature monsters who can take the form of something else, say an ordinary human. As the story progresses, this monster in human form takes part in everyday activities with other people who have no idea what he really is. But later on, we find out that what appeared to be an average guy living an average life turns out to be a scaly, ugly creature that's up to no good.

That's exactly how Satan likes to work. He can come in the form of anything he likes in order to deceive or tempt us. The form he takes depends mostly on what he knows will tempt us or cause us to give in to fear, because he knows that either of those things have the potential to separate us from God.

We often picture Satan as the comic book devil—the one with horns, a long pointed tail, a red jumpsuit, and a pitchfork. Or we think of him as a scary-looking being whose very appearance alerts us that he is pure evil. But the devil is far craftier than that. Second Corinthians 11:14 warns us that Satan "disguises himself as an angel of light." He can appear to us as something that looks good and trustworthy.

The scene in Genesis 3 demonstrates that Satan knows how to dress for success. Adam and Eve lived in the Garden among all the creatures God had created and Adam had named. Satan knew he could approach Eve in the form of one of those creatures without raising fear or suspicion. (Remember, this was a time in human history when there was no fear—no fear of snakes, spiders, or any of the beasts who lived in the Garden.) That was all a part of his plan for Eve.

And planning is something the devil is very good at.

SATAN'S GAME-PLANS FOR US

A football team spends a good part of its week of practice looking at tapes of that weekend's opponent. As the coaches and players study their opponent's game films, they watch for its strengths and weaknesses, what that team does well and not so well, and what kind of defensive and offensive formations it uses. Football teams do that so they can exploit their opponents' weaknesses and counteract their strengths. Players and coaches sometimes call this "game-planning" for an opponent.

That's what Satan does when it comes to you and me.

Because we are God's children, we can be sure that Satan has plenty of game tapes on us and that he's game-planning, looking for weaknesses he can exploit in order to take us down. He's constantly looking for ways to catch us unawares, ways to tempt us, ways to exploit our weaknesses.

THE DEVIL IS A COUNTERFEITER

One of the common tactics used by terrorists is to dress as civilians or even religious leaders, then get close enough to their targets to set off bombs and kill as many people as possible. The terrorists who do those things want to appear to be peaceful civilians, but they are counterfeits.

That is also very much like what Satan does when he wants to deceive us. He's not only a liar, but also a master counterfeiter who uses fake copies of some of God's greatest work in order to do his dirty work. Satan can make himself into a counterfeit, as he did in the Garden of Eden, and he can also perform counterfeit miracles (2 Thessalonians 2:9), as he did during the time just before the Israelites' exodus from Egypt when he copied almost perfectly some of the miracles of God. He also presents us with counterfeit doctrine (1 Timothy 4:1), with counterfeit spirits (1 John 4:1–3), with counterfeit gospels (Galatians 1:6–8), and even with a counterfeit communion (1 Corinthians 10:20–21).

And why does Satan do that? The apostle Paul answers this way: "But I am afraid that as the serpent deceived Eve by his cunning, your thoughts will be led astray from a sincere and pure devotion to Christ" (2 Corinthians 11:3). Satan loves nothing better than to take the simple message of salvation through Jesus Christ and add things to it, take things from it, and generally twist it around so that it becomes something other than what the Bible says it is.

Satan is a liar, a deceiver, and a counterfeiter. And it's important for all of us to know that he's real and that he's doing everything he can today to make our walk with Jesus and our witness for Him ineffective.

WHAT WE NEED TO KNOW

Make no mistake about it, if you are a child of God then the devil is going to be messing with you, even though you may not realize that it's him behind some of the things going on in your life. A lot of us are quick to point to physical or earthly factors as the cause for our problems. It might very well seem like your problems come from your spouse, from your children, from your boss or coworkers, or from your personality, weaknesses, or background. But you may never have made the connection between what you're going through now and the spiritual battles constantly going on around you. You may never have considered the very real possibility that the devil himself is behind the problems you face every day.

The apostle Paul pointed out the importance of making that connection when he wrote, "For we do not wrestle against flesh and blood, but against the rulers, against the authorities, against the cosmic powers over this present darkness, *against the spiritual forces of evil in the heavenly places*" (Ephesians 6:12, italics mine).

Unfortunately, many of us have bought into the lie that Satan either isn't real or that he isn't actively trying to harass us in any way he can. Because of that, we spend too much of our time fighting against flesh and blood when we should be engaging in spiritual battle with the devil and his assistants.

Those of us who haven't acknowledged what the Bible says about Satan and his role in our world today need to change our thinking. When we do that, we are one step closer to the eternal victory over evil and sin that God has promised us over and over in His written Word.

GOD IS HOLDING OUT ON YOU

Have you ever wondered if maybe, just maybe, you've given up too much in order to follow Jesus? Do you ever have this nagging feeling that in living an obedient life you're missing out on something?

If you do, you're not alone.

But that's not the way it's supposed to be. Jesus made us many wonderful promises during His time on earth, one of the most beautiful being, "I came that they may have life and have it abundantly" (John 10:10).

In making that promise, Jesus wasn't just telling us we'll have eternal life in heaven when we die. Yes, He's preparing a place for you in His everlasting kingdom, but He wants you to understand that being a Christian doesn't mean living a boring life while you wait around to go to heaven.

Sadly, a lot of believers today live their lives as if God's commandments are just His way of controlling them, of keeping them from enjoying life, of holding out on them. Too many Christians seem to think that serving Jesus simply means giving up different things. They see their faith in terms of what they are *not* to do. Somehow, they believe God is more interested in telling them what to do than in having intimate spiritual fellowship with them.

That doesn't sound like the abundant life Jesus talked about, does it? In fact, it sounds completely backward.

Is it any wonder we have so many sourpuss Christians walking around today?

When Jesus said He came to give us abundant life, He meant that He had come to provide the way for us to live in intimate fellowship with God, and that from this relationship would flow the words and actions that pleased our heavenly Father. He wants us to have exciting, joyous, victorious lives, lives that reflect Jesus Himself.

That's the kind of life Jesus wants to give us...*here and now!*

SO WHAT'S THE PROBLEM?

Jesus began His statement about coming to give us abundant life by saying, "The thief comes only to steal and kill and destroy." That thief is the devil, and his main objective for you and me is to steal our joy and make us ineffective witnesses for Christ. He is the enemy of our souls, and he'll do anything it takes to achieve that objective, including lie to us about what God really wants for us and from us.

If you've been thinking that maybe God is holding out on you and that He doesn't want you to truly enjoy life on earth, then you're buying into one of the devil's favorite lies, one he began floating all the way back in the Garden of Eden.

As the devil began his temptation of Eve, he got inside her head and tried to get her to think of God's commandments in a backward way. The first thing out of his lying mouth to Eve was, "Did God actually say, 'You shall not eat of any tree in the garden'?"

Notice that the devil started out his temptation by quoting the Word of God—more or less. That's one of Satan's favorite tricks. He loves to take the Word of God, bend it subtly, and throw it at us in the form of either a twisted truth or an outright lie. He did the same thing to

Jesus during His stay in the wilderness following His baptism (Matthew 4:1–11).

When the devil engaged Eve in conversation, he didn't just quote the Word of God, but also put it in the form of a question for Eve to consider. Satan wanted to appear to Eve as someone who really cared about her and had her best interests in mind. To that end, he twisted God's words to suit his own purposes.

If you go back and look at what God said to Adam, you'll see that Satan misquoted the Lord's real words. God never told Adam that he and Eve couldn't eat fruit from any tree in the Garden. What God *really* told them was, "From any tree of the Garden you may eat *freely*" (Genesis 2:16, NASB, italics mine).

Right off the bat, the devil threw a bald-faced lie at Eve.

God actually began His command to Adam by giving him freedom, then followed it with just one restriction: that he was not to eat from the tree of the knowledge of good and evil.

But the devil didn't want Eve focused on God-given freedom; he wanted her to focus on that one restriction. Satan wanted to take Eve's eyes off the goodness and provision of God and make her see God's regulations as proof that He wasn't quite as good to her and Adam as they might have thought. In short, the devil was telling her, "Sister, God's holding out on you. He creates you, puts you in this beautiful Garden, and then He starts off telling you what you *can't* do."

A TRIED-AND-TRUE LIE

This lie of Satan led to the fall of the entire human race, and it's the lie Satan continues to throw at us to this very day. He wants us to focus not on the goodness of God and the freedom He has given us, but on those things God has warned us not to do.

This lie worked on Eve, and I think it's safe to say it's worked on all of us at some point in our walk with Jesus.

Many of the unmarried people in my church are good examples of this. Instead of looking at all the privileges, rights, joys, and opportunities singleness gives them, so many single Christians focus instead on what they can't have righteously. A lot of these brothers and sisters are miserable, impatient people who are downright angry at God. They believe He's moving too slowly, that He's forgotten them, that He's *holding out on them* by not sending them a mate right now. Sometimes they even begin to think that this Christianity thing isn't all God says it is in His Word. Sadly, some of these young people move out ahead of God and attempt to fulfill their desires outside of His will.

If we're going to counteract the lie that God is holding out on us, we need to understand the relationship between the freedoms and the restrictions God has given us. Specifically, we need to understand that the restrictions actually lead to even *more* freedom.

I know, it sounds like a contradiction. "Restrictions lead to more freedom?" you're asking. "How could that be?" Bear with me.

So why did God put a restriction on Adam and Eve? Why couldn't Adam and Eve eat from *all* the trees in the Garden if they wanted to? Why did God put the big *not* in there? If the fruit on that one tree looked so good and so tasty—and Genesis 3:6 tells us it did—why couldn't they eat that fruit, too?

Read on, and you'll find out.

WHY *NOT*?

Those of us who live in the United States live in the freest nation on earth. We have more freedoms and more options here than in any nation that has ever existed. All you have to do to realize that is travel to other parts of the world and see how people live. In many countries, everything people do is controlled by the government. There is no freedom to choose much of anything.

But as free as we are in the U.S., our freedom is tempered by some limitations and restrictions. In western thinking, we often struggle with the idea that being told there are things we shall not do actually enhances our freedom. We don't see limitations as having anything to do with freedom. But that's exactly what our laws are designed to do. For example, I know that if I drive through a red light, I lose my freedom to drive safely and take that same freedom from others.

Every sport has its rules and limitations the participants must follow. A basketball player is free to play his own game, but he has to do it between the sidelines and endlines. And even when he stays between those lines, he is free to play his game only if he follows the rules: He can't foul his opponent and he can't run with the ball without dribbling it, just to name a few. If he steps out of bounds with the ball, there are consequences, and one of those consequences is the loss of freedom to do what he wants to do in a game.

If we were to put it in biblical language, we could say that there is a list of "You shall nots" in a basketball game. That's because having rules and limitations frees all ten players on the court to play the game as it was meant to be played. Without those rules in place, it would cease to be a basketball game and would become something else.

It's the same with the limitations God places on us. When we get it through our heads that God's regulations for life are there to enhance our own freedom, we'll go a long way toward countering Satan's lie that God is holding out on us.

THE MOST LOVING *NOT* EVER SPOKEN

We need to understand that when God gives us a prohibition against something, it is so He can give us more freedom. Sound like a contradiction? Well, it *is* something of a paradox, but there is no contradiction whatsoever about it.

Here's one example of what I'm talking about.

Speaking through Moses, God commanded His people, "You shall not covet" (Exodus 20:17). To covet is to have a consuming desire for something that doesn't belong to you. It could be that beautiful house you can't afford, that brand-new SUV in your neighbor's driveway, or the job promotion you think you deserve more than your coworker. While there's nothing necessarily wrong with desiring those kinds of things, when we allow the desires to consume us, then we've crossed the line into sin. That's why when it comes to coveting, God says one thing: Cut it out!

Now I want you to think for a moment about the freedoms God gives us when He tells us not to covet. Think about when you (or someone you know) had a consuming desire for something you couldn't have legitimately. That desire didn't bring freedom, did it? It brought nothing but anguish, anger, and jealousy.

God wants us to be free of those kinds of emotions, and that's one of the reasons He places restrictions on us.

We are free to enjoy everything we receive legitimately without guilt and without violating any of God's precepts or commandments. However, if all we see is "You shall not covet," we tend to see this commandment as confining, as God telling us that we can't have legitimate desires for things. Instead of focusing on the "no" part of a commandment, we need to flip it on its back and see the other side of "You shall not," which is "You may..."

Anything not prohibited in Scripture, by either precept or principle, is permissible for the believer. When you look around you, you see how that opens up a whole big world.

When God says no to one thing, it's because He wants to say yes to so much more. God wants to give us freedom to enjoy the blessings He gives us, but He wants us to do it in ways that enhance our intimacy with Him and benefit us most.

BLESSINGS TO *FREELY* ENJOY

As Eve began to interact with the devil concerning God's restriction on her and Adam, she told him, "We may eat of the fruit of the trees in the garden" (Genesis 3:2).

At first read, that sounds like the proper response to the devil. However, Eve left out two operative words from what God had *really* said: "From *any* tree of the garden you may eat *freely*" (Genesis 2:16, NASB, italics mine). By leaving out the words *any* and *freely*, Eve bought into Satan's lie that God was holding out on her, thus minimizing God's free provision.

So how do we overcome this satanic lie, this subversion of truth that tells us that God is holding out on us? The way I see it, it's all a matter of focus.

CHOOSING TO SEE THE POSITIVE

When Eve omitted the word *freely* from God's original commandment, she left out a key word in a lot of Scripture. When we read the word *freely* in the Bible, it almost always denotes God's grace. For example, the apostle Paul wrote that we've been "justified *freely* by his grace through the redemption that came by Christ Jesus" (Romans 3:24, NIV, italics mine). But it gets better. Later on in Romans, Paul wrote, "He [God the Father] who did not spare His own

Son, but delivered Him over for us all, how will He not also with Him *freely* give us all things?" (Romans 8:32, NASB, italics mine).

That's *all* things, folks. Not *some* things, not *most* things, but *all* things we need to live a happy, joyous life in Jesus.

There it is in writing: God desires more than anything to *freely* give us all things. He wants us to have intimate fellowship with Himself and the kind of life that flows from that kind of fellowship. That, friends, is the abundant life Jesus talked about.

CHOOSE FREEDOM

God gave Adam and Eve a choice in the Garden of Eden. He had planted all sorts of trees there, all of which were pleasing to look at and all of which bore fruit sweeter and tastier than any we could imagine. But only two of those trees are mentioned specifically: the tree of life and the tree of the knowledge of good and evil (Genesis 2:9).

The tree of life, which was one of the trees God said Adam and Eve could eat freely from, is a picture of personal fellowship with God, which we now have through Jesus Christ. That's the same kind of relationship Adam and Eve had with God before they fell into sin. The tree of the knowledge of good and evil, on the other hand, represented having to come to God based on a list of rules. The New Testament would call that the difference between grace and law. With the grace tree, you've got intimate fellowship with God based purely on the relationship itself. With the law tree, you've got a list of rules.

To put it another way, when God told Adam and Eve not to eat from the tree of the knowledge of good and evil, He wasn't holding out on them in any way. He was offering them the very best He had.

He still does today.

LIE #3

🍃

GOD CAN NOT BE TRUSTED

Eve had a decision to make. A *big* decision.

God's instructions couldn't have been any clearer. He had told Adam and Eve that they could eat from any of the trees in the Garden of Eden, except one: the tree of the knowledge of good and evil, "for in the day that you eat of it you shall surely die" (Genesis 2:17).

But as the devil conversed with Eve about what God had and hadn't said, he fed her another of his lies: "You will not surely die" (Genesis 3:4).

Earlier, I talked about how Satan loves to twist the Word of God so he can accomplish his own goals in our lives. But this time, he takes it a step further, going beyond his own spin and actually *contradicting* what God had said.

But Satan was taking it a step beyond contradicting this one commandment. What he was really telling Eve was that she shouldn't believe what God had clearly said. He was telling her that God's Word can not be trusted. He was, in effect, calling God a liar.

THE DEVIL: BOLD IN HIS LIES

Satan is crafty and smart and knows how to push our buttons. But there's another side of the enemy we need to understand: He's very bold. The devil knew that God was the Creator of the universe, the Creator of the devil himself. He knew that it was God who had kicked him out of heaven, and he knew that he had been sentenced to eternal fire.

Yet here he was, calling the God who had done all those things a liar!

Eve was faced with a serious question: Who was she going to believe? Was she going to believe what God had said, or was she going to believe the devil? There was no room for compromise here. It was an either/or situation for Eve.

That's the very same question we are faced with daily.

Will we believe God and take Him at His Word, or will we join the devil in holding that God's Word can't be trusted?

A DECISION WE ALL HAVE TO MAKE

The thought of telling God that His Word can't be trusted should send shivers down the spine of every believer. After all, this whole Christian thing is built around faith, around believing that God keeps the promises He has made in His Word.

Can you think of a time when you might have joined the devil in saying that God's Word can't be trusted? Off the top of our heads, most of us would probably respond, "God forbid! I'd never say that the Word of God is anything but true and trustworthy." However, I believe that just about every Christian at some point or another has done that through words and deeds.

This may sound harsh, but many people's lives reflect an unwillingness to take God at His Word. Our churches are full of professing believers who treat the Word of God as if they were atheists.

When our lives reflect an unwillingness or inability to acknowledge the Word of God as truth, the devil has us right where he wants us. But the good news is that we *can* trust God and believe every word He has spoken.

A Word You Can Trust

The Bible is filled with promise after fulfilled promise about the trustworthiness of God's Word. Jesus Himself spoke about this when He said, "For truly, I say to you, until heaven and earth pass away, not an iota, not a dot, will pass from the Law until all is accomplished" (Matthew 5:18).

In short, if the Bible says it, we can bank on it.

But there is more to our faith than simply agreeing with God that His Word can be trusted. We must put some kind of action behind that faith. Jesus defined that action when he told a group of His disciples, "'If you abide in my word, you are truly my disciples, and you will know the truth, and the truth will set you free'" (John 8:31–32).

Now let's turn that around and look at another implication of what Jesus said: If we don't know the truth of God's Word, then we will be in bondage.

A lot of believers are in serious bondage today. They've received Jesus Christ as their Lord and Savior, and they do their best to live the way God wants them to. But Satan has a field day with them, keeping them in mental, emotional, and spiritual chains, because while they may acknowledge the power and truth of God's Word, their actions say that they've bought into Satan's lie that the Word can't be trusted.

When Jesus told us to abide in His Word, He meant that we are to hold to it, to make it a part of our being, to have faith that every word of it is true and profitable for us.

YA GOTTA HAVE FAITH

The first thing we need to know about our God is that it is absolutely 100 percent outside of God's nature for Him to lie (Hebrews 6:18). God couldn't lie even if He wanted to. When He speaks, we can know that what He says is absolute truth, nothing more and nothing less.

Taking God at His Word requires just one thing: faith. I'm not going to get all theological on you now as I define what faith is. Rather, I'm just going to tell you that faith means believing that God keeps His promises. The writer of Hebrews put it this way: "Now faith is the assurance of things hoped for, the conviction of things not seen" (Hebrews 11:1).

Having faith means we don't have to see something to know it's true. For example, I am confident that I have an eternal home in heaven, not because I've been there or seen it but because I believe God. Jesus promised the disciples, "In my Father's house are many rooms. If it were not so, would I have told you that I go to prepare a place for you? And if I go and prepare a place for you, I will come again and will take you to myself, that where I am you may be also" (John 14:2–3).

As the old saying goes, "God said it, I believe it, and that settles it."

If I didn't believe God's Word, I would have no confidence in heaven or anything else He has promised. I know that unless Jesus returns in the next few decades, I'm going to die. But I'm not afraid of dying because I know that death means that I'll be ushered into the presence of my heavenly Father.

When we settle in our hearts and minds that God's Word can be trusted, we solve a lot of problems in our lives. We believe that He'll provide for us, that He'll guide us, that He'll love us with an everlasting love, and that we have an eternal home with Him.

We know these things by faith when we know the substance and character of the One promising them. Our faith is in a *real* God who has made us *real* promises. We can't have faith in the promises of the Easter Bunny or Santa Claus because neither of them is real. However, our God is real and so we can believe His Word—every bit of it.

Now, let's take a look at how we effectively counter Satan's lie that God can't be trusted. We'll do that by looking at the Word itself.

THE WORD AS A WEAPON

The apostle Paul, writing to a young protégé of his named Timothy, said, "All Scripture is breathed out by God and profitable for teaching, for reproof, for correction, and for training in righteousness, that the man of God may be competent, equipped for every good work" (2 Timothy 3:16–17).

Paul wanted Timothy to understand something that we need to understand today. All Scripture—every word of it—is profitable for us. If we want to learn God's character, we go to the Bible. If we want to make changes in our lives, we look to the Scriptures. If we want to live righteous lives before God, we find out how by reading the Word of God.

But did you know that the Bible also encourages us to use the Word of God as a weapon against Satan?

In the book of Ephesians, Paul encouraged believers to "put on the whole armor of God, that you may be able to stand against the schemes of the devil" (Ephesians 6:11). Paul uses interesting imagery in this passage, encouraging us to "fasten on the belt of truth," "put on the breastplate of righteousness," "as shoes for your feet, having put on the readiness given by the gospel of peace," and "take up the shield of faith...and the helmet of salvation." Finally, Paul says we are to "take...the sword of the Spirit, which is the *word of God*" (6:17, italics mine).

Every piece of the "full armor of God," except one, is a defensive implement meant to help us ward off the attacks of the devil. Paul refers to the Word of God as a sword, a weapon of offense. That tells us that we need to go on the offensive against the devil, and that we can use the Word as a weapon.

The devil is the most intelligent of all created beings, so he isn't afraid of your intellect, wisdom, or your life experiences. He's also not afraid of your influence, your power, or your gifts and abilities. You can't impress or intimidate the devil on your own. But there is one weapon at your disposal that he absolutely can't handle, and that's the Word of God.

But how do we use the Word of God as a weapon? In Matthew 4, we see the perfect example.

"IT IS WRITTEN..."

Jesus had just finished a forty-day fast in the wilderness outside Jerusalem. After not eating for forty days, Jesus was in some ways at the most vulnerable stage in His ministry. The devil knew that if he had any shot at steering Jesus away from the purpose for which He had come to earth, it was now.

The devil knew exactly what would be most tempting to a man who hadn't eaten in over a month, so he said to Jesus, "If you are the Son of God, command these stones to become loaves of bread" (4:3). But Jesus knew that doing a miracle like that at the devil's request was not part of God's program.

Jesus didn't debate the devil or try to outwit him. He didn't just try harder or pray harder. Rather, He simply spoke the Word of God to counter the devil: "It is written, 'Man shall not live by bread alone, but by every word that comes from the mouth of God'" (4:4).

But the devil wasn't about to give up. He knew that eternity hung in the balance, so he came back at Jesus. Satan took Jesus to the highest point of the temple in Jerusalem and said, "If you are the Son of God, throw yourself down, for it is written, 'He will command his angels concerning you,' and 'On their hands they will bear you up, lest you strike your foot against a stone'" (4:6).

Once again, there's the devil quoting God, but with his own demented, evil twist. And once again, Jesus answered with His Word: "Again it is written, 'You shall not put the Lord your God to the test'" (4:7).

Finally, Satan got down to what he really wanted all along. He took Jesus to a high mountain, showed Him the kingdoms and pleasures of the world, and said, "All these I will give you, if you will fall down and worship me" (4:9). By now, Jesus was finished with the devil. He said, "Be gone, Satan! For it is written, 'You shall worship the Lord your God and him only shall you serve'" (4:10).

Every word Jesus spoke was from the written Word of God, which Jesus had spent His life studying and learning to apply. Jesus knew then what we need to know today: The devil has no answer for the true Word of God spoken in faith. When the devil heard Jesus counterattack him by speaking God's Word, he did the only thing he could do: leave!

He'll do the same when we use the Word of God against him.

Is it any wonder, then, that Satan wants more than anything for us to believe that God's Word can't be trusted?

TIME TO TAKE UP YOUR SWORD

A lot of Christians today spend their lives fighting a losing battle with the devil. They pray, go to church, and even read their Bibles daily. But Satan is still there harassing them and making their walk with Jesus anything but victorious and abundant.

I believe this is because so many of us don't do as Paul instructed us and as Jesus demonstrated and use the Word as a weapon of offense against Satan. They may know what the Bible says and even apply it to their personal lives the best they can, but they don't pick it up as an ancient warrior would have picked up his sword as he headed out for battle.

We have an absolutely devastating weapon to use against Satan and his lies. But that weapon is useful only if we take the time to pick it up.

It may shock you to know this, but the devil knows more about God's Word than any of us do. Not only that, he's amazingly crafty when it comes to using it against us when he has the chance. Spiritual battle is difficult enough as it is, but if we don't know enough Scripture, we'll have no chance against the devil.

In order to use the Word of God to defeat the devil, we need to do the things necessary to know the Scriptures. That means reading, studying, and meditating on the Bible *daily*. When we do that, we'll be ready when the devil throws lies and temptations our way. No longer will we be like so many believers, standing there looking like a deer in the headlights. We'll know what to do and what to say to the devil.

That's the opposite of what happened to Eve. Satan saw that she didn't know God's Word—she couldn't even recite it to him correctly—so he knew she would be an easy mark.

WE'VE GOT IT IN WRITING

One time, my car broke down and I was stranded—I mean *really* stranded. I didn't have AAA at the time, so I called everybody I knew to come pick me up, but I could reach no one. Finally, after I'd spent hours sitting in my car waiting, someone came to pick me up and tow my car.

Later, I was telling a friend about this unpleasant episode, and he asked me, "Have you looked at your driver's license?" I told him I'd looked at my driver's license lots of times. "No," he said, "have you really *looked* at your driver's license?"

I had no idea where he was going with his question, so I pulled out my license. As I looked at it, my friend told me to take a look at the back of the card. There it was—the number for Texas Roadside Assistance, which was set up for drivers in the same predicament I'd found myself in. I'd sat in my car for hours, getting frustrated and tired, when all I had to do was call a number I had on me the whole time, then wait for the cavalry to arrive.

A lot of believers feel far worse frustration in their lives than I felt that day my car broke down. They feel stuck and they don't know what to do. Sadly, many of them have never taken the time to read what's already been written to answer their questions, ease their frustrations, and provide the weapon they need to fight off the devil. It's all right there in the pages of the Bible.

From the first word of Genesis to the last word of Revelation, God's Word is true and trustworthy. All we need to do is obey the words of Jesus and abide in that Word and we'll have an answer for any lie or temptation Satan throws our way.

LIE #4

SIN CARRIES NO CONSEQUENCES

We've all seen the "No Trespassing" signs private property owners post to let outsiders know they are not welcome. But many of those signs also contain this ominous warning: "Violators Will Be Prosecuted."

There are always consequences when we break the law, and that is especially true when it comes to God's law. While our Christian faith is built around a relationship, God has also put in place His own "No Trespassing" signs in the form of His law and has also warned us that there are consequences for breaking that law.

However, the devil wants us to believe that we can sin without suffering the consequences. Like so many of his lies, this one started out in the Garden of Eden.

Once Satan had engaged Eve in conversation, she told him that she and Adam had been forbidden from eating "of the tree that is in the midst of the garden." Eve went on to tell Satan that God had said, "You shall not eat of the fruit of the tree...neither shall you touch it, lest you die" (Genesis 3:3).

Remember, Eve didn't have what God said completely right. And the fact that she had misquoted the Word gave Satan the opening he needed, and he told her, "You will not surely die" (Genesis 3:4).

The devil's message was as devious as it was simple, and it's a lie he throws at God's people today: Sin has no consequences.

But God wants us to know two things: He takes sin very seriously and He can not allow sin to go unpunished.

THE SERIOUSNESS OF SIN

As a prank, some students at a college snatched the mascot—a goat—from the campus of a nearby rival school. After they had the goat in their custody, they were faced with the problem of where to keep it. When two of the students volunteered to keep the animal in their dorm room, someone asked about the smell. The two answered, "Don't worry, the goat will get used to it."

It's amazing how some people can get used to the stench they live in. But we need to know that God will never get used to the stench of sin in our lives. Because God is completely holy, meaning that He is separate and unique and can not be in the presence of unrighteousness, He will never adapt Himself to sin. While we as fallen human beings can easily get used to sin, God can not.

But what exactly is sin? The Bible defines sin as anything and everything that is contrary to the holiness of God. In a nutshell, sin is violation of the laws and regulations of God, who has put those laws and regulations in place to reflect for us His character and His holiness.

We must clearly understand that violating God's laws always carries with it consequences. As the apostle Paul put it, "Do not be deceived: God is not mocked, for whatever one sows, that will he also reap. For the one who sows to his own flesh will from the flesh reap corruption" (Galatians 6:7).

The basic truth that sin always comes with consequences was demonstrated in the Garden of Eden, where Adam and Eve both suffered for what they had done.

THE *REAL* CONSEQUENCES OF SIN

God had said explicitly that on the day Adam and Eve ate from the tree of the knowledge of good and evil they would certainly die (Genesis 2:17). But while we know that sin led to the deterioration of Adam and Eve's bodies and ultimately to physical death, we also know that they both lived for many, many decades after they sinned.

At a glance, it might look as if God's warnings that the man and his wife would die if they disobeyed hadn't come true. But when we look at what really happened to them, we see that they died in many ways the very day they chose to sin.

In the Bible, the word *death* doesn't always refer to physical dying but sometimes points to separation from God and what follows that separation. When God said that the man and woman would surely die if they ate the forbidden fruit, it meant that they would be separated and alienated from Him. It meant that an impregnable barrier would be placed between them and Him from that day forward.

The sad truth is that Adam and Eve's sin led to a multiplicity of deaths, all of which are recorded in Genesis 3:

They died spiritually. Before Adam and Eve sinned, they enjoyed free and guiltless fellowship with God. But after they sinned, it was a different picture: "And they heard the sound of the LORD God walking in the garden in the cool of the day, and the man and his wife hid themselves from the presence of the LORD God among the trees of the garden" (Genesis 3:8).

After Adam and Eve fell, they actually felt the need to *hide* from God. When we feel the need to hide from our Creator rather than enjoy intimacy with Him, it is because spiritual death has taken place, because sin has created a wall between us and Him.

They died emotionally. God never intended for Adam and Eve to know fear, guilt, and shame, but following their sin, we see all three emotions in Adam's response to God: "I heard the sound of you in the garden, and I was afraid, because I was naked, and I hid myself" (Genesis 3:10).

Where before, Adam and Eve had walked around the garden completely naked and felt no guilt, fear, or shame, now they are filled with all three. Adam and Eve died emotionally that day, just as you and I die emotionally when we sin. God wants us to be able to approach Him boldly and enjoy being in His presence. Unfortunately, many believers aren't able to do that because of their own emotional difficulties—depression, anxiety, fear, and guilt—which many are quick to attribute to psychological problems. While those can be very real problems in the lives of believers, I believe they are often rooted in our own sin.

They died relationally. Sin results in all kinds of relational problems, including marital conflict, name-calling, and finger-pointing. We see that in Adam's rationalization of his sin: "The woman whom you gave to be with me, she gave me fruit of the tree, and I ate" (Genesis 3:12).

It was no accident that Satan chose to go to Eve first as he attempted to bring about the fall of humankind. The devil knew that God had set up the family so that Adam would be the leader, the one charged with the responsibility of overseeing the Garden (Genesis 2:15, 23–24), and that he was given God's first commandment to humankind (Genesis 2:17). The devil knew that bypassing Adam, who was supposed to lead, and going to Eve, would throw the whole man/woman relationship—and all relationships that followed—into chaos.

They died economically. Before Adam and Eve fell into sin, Adam was more of a groundskeeper than a laborer. It was work, but it was work God blessed and made successful. But as a consequence of sin, work took on a completely different look:

"Because you have listened to the
voice of your wife and have eaten of the tree

of which I commanded you,
'You shall not eat from it,'
cursed is the ground because of you;
in pain you shall eat of it
all the days of your life; thorns and thistles it shall
bring forth for you;
and you shall eat the plants of the field.
By the sweat of your face
you shall eat bread,
till you return to the ground,
for out of it you were taken;
for you are dust,
and to dust you shall return."

GENESIS 3:17–19

Many people believe they are miserable at work because they don't like their boss or because the work they do seems so unfulfilling. But the truth is, as a consequence of sin the whole world of work remains cursed to this day.

They died directionally. Before sin entered the picture, Adam and Eve didn't have to worry about choices. They had only one direction to go: whatever direction God was taking them. But when they chose to sin against God, "the eyes of both were opened" (Genesis 3:7). Adam and Eve had more information than they were intended to have. They now knew what sin and evil were.

"But how can we be worse off with more information?" you may ask. Simply because in some ways, more information means less innocence. When a baby is born, the only thing he knows is that Mom is there for him. But as he grows and matures, he has more choices and more information to work with. In time, he'll have to choose what is right and wrong. Before the Fall, Adam and Eve never had to worry about that choice.

It didn't take long for Satan's lie that sin has no consequences to be exposed, did it? On the very day that Adam and Eve sinned against their God, they suffered the consequences, consequences humankind suffers from to this day.

THE CERTAINTY—AND UNCERTAINTY— OF CONSEQUENCES

When we choose to sin, there *will* be consequences. However, that's where our choice in the matter ends. We choose to sin, but God is the One who chooses the consequences. He decides what happens because of our sin, how many times it will happen, and how long it will last.

Some consequences flow directly out of our sin. If we choose to engage in sexual sin, we may very well suffer the consequences of an unwanted pregnancy or disease. That kind of sin carries with it natural consequences, the kind that God put in place long ago.

But there is another kind of consequences for sin, the ones that God Himself actively brings on us when we sin against Him.

A lot of people have difficulty believing that God brings consequences into our lives because of our sin. "How could God do that?" they ask. "I thought He loved me?" But as the writer of the book of Hebrews tells us, God does discipline us, and He does it *because* of His deep love:

> It is for discipline that you have to endure. God is treating you as sons. For what son is there whom his father does not discipline? If you are left without discipline, in which all have participated, then you are illegitimate children and not sons. Besides this, we have had earthly fathers who disciplined us and we respected them. Shall we not much more be subject to the Father of spirits and live? For they disciplined us for a short time as it seemed best to them, but he disciplines us for our good, that we may share his holiness.
>
> HEBREWS 12:7–10

I remember times when my father punished me for my disobedience, and I now understand that he didn't punish me because he enjoyed it but because he wanted me to understand how important it was that I obey him.

God doesn't enjoy punishing us either. But when He takes out His belt to give us a "spanking," He does it because He loves us and wants us to understand the importance of obedience. That, Hebrews 12:10 tells us, is so we "may share his holiness."

Being disciplined by God this way isn't fun, but He has assured us that it is for our own good. As Hebrews 12 continues, we see that, "For the moment all discipline seems painful rather than pleasant, but later it yields the peaceful fruit of righteousness to those who have been trained by it" (v. 11).

When God metes out the consequences for our sin in the form of punishment or discipline, we can take comfort in knowing that He not only knows how much is needed, but also that He always follows it with restoration and redemption.

One of Jesus' best-known parables shows us beautifully how that works.

Restoring and Redeeming a Wayward Child

The Parable of the Prodigal Son (Luke 15:11–32) is a wonderful illustration of how God allows calamity in the life of His beloved, waits for repentance, then lovingly welcomes His wayward child back into His fold.

The prodigal son did something many of us would think foolish. He asked his father, a very wealthy man, for his share of his inheritance, then left the family estate and traveled to another country, where he blew all his money on loose living.

Eventually, his decision to leave his father took him to a point lower than he could ever have imagined. He was broke and no one was hiring, so in order to survive, he took work feeding pigs, animals the Jews considered unclean and wouldn't even touch. He was so hungry that even the slop he was feeding the pigs looked good.

Finally, as this young man stood in the filth and stench of the pigpen, he "came to his senses" (Luke 15:17, NASB). It dawned on him that even his father's servants had it better than he did. So he came up with a plan: He would go back to his father, confess that he had sinned, and ask if he could stay around as a hired hand.

The young man set out to do just that. He went home and told his father, "I have sinned against heaven and before you. I am no longer worthy to be called your son" (Luke 15:21). But the father wasn't having any of this nonsense about taking him on as his hired hand. This young man was his son, and because he had returned home and repented, his father took him back with open arms and threw him a huge welcome-home bash, "for this my son was dead, and is alive again; he was lost, and is found" (Luke 15:24).

This young man's repentance was the result of his being broken. He had suffered through the consequences of his sin before he was humbled and ready to return home. Notice too that it involved returning somewhere—back home to his father—and verbally acknowledging that he had sinned.

Repentance doesn't mean just feeling sorry for what we've done. It involves action. It means moving back toward God, humbly confessing our sin to Him, and receiving His forgiveness and restoration. When we do these things, God welcomes us back to Himself, forgives our sin, and redeems what we've lost when we were away from Him.

Sin always has consequences, despite what Satan tries

to tell us. But the good news is that God's grace is greater than any sin we can commit. God has warned us that sin always leads to death of some kind, but He also promises that He is "faithful and just to forgive us our sins and to cleanse us from all unrighteousness" (1 John 1:9).

LIE #5

YOU CAN BE LIKE GOD

Several years ago, there were a series of television commercials for the sports drink Gatorade starring Michael Jordan, the greatest basketball player ever to lace up a pair of sneakers. The ads showed a series of shots of Michael doing his thing, while the singers in the background sang, "I wanna be like Mike."

I think it's safe to say that there's not a basketball player around who wouldn't want to be like Michael Jordan. But you can drink all the Gatorade you can stand, wear the most expensive Nike basketball shoes made, have on a

Chicago Bulls jersey with number 23 on it 24/7, and you will still never be like Mike. Why? Because as a basketball player, Michael Jordan was in a class all his own.

Those commercials appealed to something in every human heart, namely the desire to be something we can never be, no matter what we eat, drink, or wear. That's the same part of Eve's heart that the devil appealed to when he uttered his lie: "You will be like God."

So You Wanna Be Like God...

Satan had already fed Eve a raft of lies, one of which was that there would be no consequences if she chose to eat the forbidden fruit. But he took his deception a step further when he told her that not only would she not die if she ate but that there were amazing benefits if she did: "For God knows that when you eat of it your eyes will be opened, and you will be like God, knowing good and evil" (Genesis 3:5).

There was a kernel of truth in what the devil said. As I pointed out before, when Adam and Eve ate from the tree of the knowledge of good and evil, they immediately became aware of sin and evil. The big lie, however, was that Eve would be like God if she ate from the tree.

In God's written Word, the Bible, He has told us repeatedly that there is only one God, and that no one had ever been like Him and no one ever would be—no angel, no devil, no human being.

God is in a class by Himself, and He is so protective of His own identity that He commanded the people of Israel not to make any replica or likeness of Him (Exodus 20:4). One of the reasons God commanded the people not to make a likeness of Him is that no picture they could draw or statue they could carve could capture God as He really is.

Speaking through the Old Testament prophet Isaiah, God repeatedly declared His uniqueness:

> "You are my witnesses," declares the LORD,
> "and my servant whom I have chosen,
> that you may know and believe me
> and understand that I am he.
> Before me no God was formed,
> nor shall there be any after me."
>
> ISAIAH 43:10

> Thus says the LORD, the King of Israel
> and his Redeemer, the LORD of hosts:
> "I am the first and I am the last;
> besides me there is no god.
> Who is like me? Let him proclaim it.

Let him declare and set it before me,
since I appointed an ancient people.
Let them declare what is to come,
and what will happen."

ISAIAH 44:6–7

"I am the LORD, and there is no other,
besides me there is no God;
I equip you, though you do not know me."

ISAIAH 45:5

The bottom line in God's words through Isaiah? There
is only one God, and we're not it!

HE'S GOD, WE'RE NOT

The most important thing the devil left out of his lie that
Adam and Eve could be "like God" was that there is an infinite difference between the Creator (God) and the created
(humankind). But the devil turned that truth around on
Eve, telling her, in essence, that she could reach her full
potential only if she did the one thing that would make her
more like God.

One of the reasons God placed that one limitation on
Adam and Eve was to remind them of who was who, to

draw a line between the Creator and the created. God wanted it to be clear that there was a big difference between Himself and humankind.

He wanted Adam and Eve—and every human who would live after them—to understand that:

- He is transcendent, meaning that He surpasses every*thing* and every*one* in power and authority.
- He is infinite in His knowledge, while they are limited in what they know.
- He is eternal and unlimited by time, while they as created beings are not.
- His nature and attributes, those things that make Him God, make it in their best interests to obey the one and only restriction He has put in place for them.

All humans from Adam and Eve on are limited in a number of ways. We have a beginning and are finite—finite in our time to live, in our knowledge, and in our wisdom. Because we are limited in all these ways, God had to put boundaries and limitations on us. But because God Himself is infinite, He is not limited in any way. There are no boundaries or limitations governing or restraining Him other than His own nature and character.

This is why God in His wisdom knew that it was necessary to make such a vivid distinction between Himself and His children.

THE NEED FOR THE DISTINCTION

Those who have teenagers at home have a live-in illustration of how people tend to want to erase distinctions (in that case the distinction between parent and child). A good parent knows that all freedoms a child enjoys must be tempered with limitations. For example, you can give your teen the freedom to go out and enjoy time with his friends, but you give him the restriction to be home by a certain, predetermined time. But teenagers, being teenagers, want to push things. When you say, "Be in by midnight," they often push it to 12:15, then to 12:30. After a while the line between parent and teen can become blurred.

God never intended for the distinction between Himself and His people to be blurred in any way. Yes, He wanted to have a loving, intimate relationship with His creation. He wanted to be able to walk with us, laugh with us, and love on us. It was going to be the perfect relationship, one where we were innocently dependant on our heavenly Father for everything we need and everything we are.

That included what we were to know and how we were to know it.

THE TRUTH WE WERE NEVER MEANT TO HANDLE

In the movie *A Few Good Men*, there is a now-legendary exchange between a U.S. Marine Corps Colonel named Nathan R. Jessep, played by Jack Nicholson, and a U.S. Navy prosecutor named Lt. Daniel Kaffee, played by Tom Cruise. Near the end of Jessep's time on the witness stand in a court martial hearing, Kaffee, frustrated at Jessep's evasive attitude toward his questioning, shouts, "I want the truth!" Jessep angrily bellows back, "You can't handle the truth!"

Colonel Jessep wanted Kaffee to believe that there were some things he just shouldn't know about, things he couldn't handle if he knew them. Sometimes ignorance truly is bliss.

Satan wanted Eve to believe that God had put a limitation on her in order to keep her in ignorance. He wanted her to believe that God was keeping her and Adam from knowing the difference between good and evil so He could control her and tell her what to do.

But God is not a God who wants us to live in ignorance. On the contrary, He wants us to grow in knowledge.

God wanted Adam and Eve to learn as they lived—learn to walk in perfect love and obedience, learn to love one another, and even learn how to take good care of the most magnificent garden ever planted. But He wanted them to learn while maintaining a sense of dependence on Him. In His wisdom, God knew that His created beings did not have what it took to handle the knowledge of evil. He created them to live in perfect harmony with Him, not to be separate and independent from Him.

But of course, Satan couldn't leave that alone. He was in all-out rebellion against God, and he was going to do anything and everything he could to mess with that perfect union between God and man.

And at the heart of Satan's lie that Eve could be "like God, knowing good and evil" was the lie that humankind can live and think independently from God, that we could have complete autonomy from God while still enjoying the blessings He has given.

AUTONOMY FROM GOD?

A man once asked three of his friends—a psychologist, an accountant, and a lawyer—"What is the meaning of truth?" The psychologist answered first, telling him, "Truth is what you *feel* it to be." The second answer came from the accountant: "Truth is what you *need* it to be." The third and final answer came from the lawyer, who said, "Truth is what you *can make* it to be."

That's what happens when we claim autonomy from God. Apart from God, humankind can not come up with absolute truth. Sure, we can come up with some great scientific discoveries and inventions, and we can make amazing strides in curing disease. But when it comes to knowing real and complete truth, we are hopelessly lost.

Satan intended that Adam and Eve do more than just possess the knowledge of good and evil. He also wanted them to make it their responsibility to choose for themselves what good and evil were. He wanted their limited minds to think independently of an eternal and infinitely wise Creator, who alone possessed absolute truth.

The devil wants the same for humanity to this very day.

The appeal of modern secular humanism is that humans can live and think independently of God, that eventually our knowledge and wisdom will allow us to solve all of our problems, that we will overcome evil and create our own utopia, our own Garden of Eden. In short, we can be our own god.

However, the psalmist shows us the Lord's response to the idea of human autonomy from the true and living God:

Why do the nations rage
and the peoples plot in vain?
The kings of the earth set themselves,
and the rulers take counsel together,
against the Lord and against his anointed, saying,
"Let us burst their bonds apart
and cast away their cords from us."
He who sits in the heavens laughs;
the Lord holds them in derision.

PSALM 2:1–4

It hasn't taken secular humanism long to show that it can't even solve the problem of where we and our world came from, let alone how we'll solve our life problems. Human science apart from God has attempted to explain how our earth came into existence and how we got here. One of those theories is called the "Big Bang," and it holds that a huge cosmic explosion started the universe. But no one has been able to explain exactly what went *bang* in the first place.

Satan's lie that humankind can live and think independently of its Creator is both wicked and destructive. But it gets worse. You see, what the devil was offering Eve wasn't truly autonomy and independence. What he was *really* offering was a choice between dependence on the true and living Creator of the universe or dependence on what the apostle Paul called "the god of this world" (2 Corinthians 4:4), the devil himself.

A BIG CHOICE TO MAKE

The devil told Eve that if she would just take a nibble of the forbidden fruit, she would be like God, *knowing...* But what he didn't tell Eve was that if she chose to eat, she was obeying the devil himself, and not her Creator. The devil was not just offering her knowledge independent of God; he was also offering her himself as her new god.

Remember, the devil wanted more than anything to be like God (Isaiah 14:13–14). And while he knew that Adam and Eve couldn't really be like God, he knew he could separate them from Him and throw all of creation into chaos if he could just get the man and woman to do the one thing God told them not to do. And he also knew that in his own twisted way, he could take dominion in this world, giving him the chance to cause turmoil, division, and death—at least for as long as God allowed it.

To this day, whom we obey will determine whom we're subordinate to. *Someone* will be calling the shots in our lives. If we hear the lies of the devil and obey him, then we are in bondage to him. But when we make ourselves subordinate to our loving Creator, we get to live in the blessings and freedom and love He has so richly poured out on us.

God loves us so deeply that He allows us to make that very choice. Our God isn't One to force anyone to love Him or obey Him. He wants our obedience and love for Him to come from willing, humble hearts. He wants us to see that He is a good and gracious and loving heavenly Father who had the very best for us at heart when He gave us boundaries and limitations to live by.

When Satan came whispering his lies in Eve's ear, she had a decision to make, one with ramifications stretching all the way through eternity. So do we. The choice we have to make is who we're going to obey and follow. Who will call the shots in our lives?

The true and living God, the One who lives from eternity to eternity, desires more than anything that we humble ourselves and make Him our personal, one-and-only God. When we do that, He comes to us and lives within us, gives us direction, and teaches us His ultimate truth.

He really is one of a kind, isn't He?

LIE #6

IF IT FEELS GOOD, DO IT!

Back in the early seventies, comic Flip Wilson gained wild popularity as host of his own television program. Part of what made the show so popular was Wilson's characters, including Geraldine, a blunt-talking, respect-demanding, no-guff-taking black woman who always used the same excuse when she did something she knew was wrong: "The devil made me do it!"

That line made a lot of us laugh and became a national fad for a time, but it's hardly based in truth. You see, the devil can't *make* us do anything, and he knows it. He knows that God created us with a free will. We make our own choices when it comes to what we do and don't do and whom we follow.

What the devil can do, however, is suggest things to us, coerce us, and deceive us into making wrong or sinful choices. Just as a clever advertisement can make us desire anything from a new car to a specific brand of toothpaste, the devil can turn our eyes toward sin.

The devil is good at this tactic. He's been doing it for thousands of years, starting way back in the Garden. The devil knew he couldn't force Eve to do anything, so he coerced and deceived her by creating in her mind a false image of God and of the command He had given.

In short, he replaced her focus on God's words "you shall not," to his own, "If it feels good, do it!"

A NEW AND MUDDLED PERSPECTIVE

There can be little doubt that Eve had seen the tree of the knowledge of good and evil. She and Adam had daily walked with God in Eden, and since the tree was planted in the middle of the Garden (Genesis 2:9), it's hard to imagine her missing it.

But now, with the devil's lies fresh in Eve's mind, the tree somehow looked different. She was looking at it through the devil's lie-colored glasses rather than through the clear lens of God's truth. Finally, all of Satan's lies were culminated in a new focus on the tree: "So when the woman saw that the tree was good for food, and that it was a delight to the eyes, and that the tree was to be desired to make one wise" (Genesis 3:6).

To Eve, it all *felt* right. She was going to do it! As the second part of Genesis 3:6 tells us, "she took of its fruit and ate, and she also gave some to her husband who was with her, and he ate."

THE PROBLEM WITH FEELING

Eve wasn't looking for sin the day the devil appeared to tempt her. She didn't wake up that morning thinking of what she could do to ruin her and Adam's lives and throw all of Creation into turmoil. She didn't have to—sin came looking for her, just as it comes looking for us daily.

The devil came at Eve, using one of God's gifts to humankind: feelings.

We need to understand some things about feelings, starting with the fact that God created them and gave us the capacity to have them, just as He Himself has feelings. In the Bible, we see examples of how God feels pleasure, joy, anger, and sadness, just to name a few emotions. He gave us the ability to feel all those things.

We also need to understand that while feelings are a gift from God, they have limitations. Feelings are vastly different from thoughts. They can be real and powerful, but they don't operate the same way as rational thinking. Feelings can go up and down, while what we know to be truth stays the same. Feelings tend to react, while thinking tends to keep itself grounded in what we know.

If you were to see a horror movie, you might feel scared. When you look up at the screen and see a monster jump out from behind a door, you jump, your heart rate picks up, and your palms start to sweat. When you do those things, you're reacting emotionally, and as your startle reflex, your increased heart rate, and your sweaty palms show, those feelings are real. But in your rational mind, you know the truth: The monster on the screen isn't real.

The bottom line is that feelings can react to something we know not to be true.

That's why, when it comes to responding to what God tells us, we must put what we *know* ahead of what we *feel*. We must make our knowledge of His truth the engine and our feelings the caboose. We need to make sure that our feelings are guided by what we know, not the other way around.

Satan turned the caboose of Eve's feelings into the engine and her knowledge into the caboose. He wanted her to use the emotions he had stirred up in her to make her choice about whether to eat or not to eat. He wanted her to *feel* as though she couldn't trust God's Word, *feel* that God was holding out on her, *feel* that there would be no consequences, but only the benefit of being "like God" if she chose to disobey.

THE MORE THINGS CHANGE...

Thousands of years after the scene in the Garden, the apostle John wrote this of the sinful pleasures the world has to offer: "For all that is in the world, the lust of the flesh and the lust of the eyes and the boastful pride of life, is not from the Father, but is from the world" (1 John 2:16, NASB).

When you compare this verse with Genesis 3:6, you'll notice some striking parallels. John tells us that the world offers:

- the lust of the flesh (the fruit looked good for Eve to eat)
- the lust of the eyes (the fruit was pleasing to Eve's eyes)

- the boastful pride of life (the fruit was desirable to make Eve wise).

Satan knew then and he knows now that he can appeal to these kinds of feelings, which are in the heart of every human. Each of us wants to satisfy the lusts of our flesh and of our eyes, and each of us wants to think more highly of ourselves than God says we should.

I'm not going to lie: Sin feels good. A lot of preachers will tell you that sin really isn't that much fun, that you can't really enjoy doing what is wrong. But we all know that a lot of things God tells us not to do can be, at least for a season, very enjoyable. The devil knows that too, and he knows how to whisper his lies about how we should do what we want if it feels good to us.

But as he does with so many of his lies, he leaves out the part he doesn't want us to know before we choose to sin—that the pleasures of sin, though they may *feel* very real to us, are in the long run nothing but illusion.

THE ILLUSION OF "IF IT FEELS GOOD, DO IT!"

When my kids were little, I'd often sit them in my lap in the car and let them put their little hands on the steering wheel while I drove around the church parking lot. They would get so excited, thinking they were actually driving the car. But my children were under an illusion. They weren't driving at all; I was in control the whole time.

Sometimes a little illusion like that can be fun. But there is one illusion that is anything but fun, and it's the one that says we're in control when we buy into Satan's lie, "If it feels good, do it!"

Part of the devil's strategy in getting us to sin is to give us the illusion that we can control it. For a while, it even seems that way. We do what feels good thinking we're in control, but it's only a matter of time before sin controls us.

If you were to talk to anyone whose marriage, ministry, or life has been ruined by the effects of drugs, alcohol, pornography, or any other addiction, I think that person would tell you, "I never thought it would come to this." I've known many people who dabbled in sin—a little bit of drinking, pornography, or "harmless" flirtation outside their marriage—only to find that there came a time when they couldn't control it any more. They were no longer playing with sin; sin was playing with them.

What Satan didn't want Eve to know—and what he doesn't want us to know today—is that when we decide to disobey God, when we remove ourselves from the protection of God, then the devil is running the show. And when the devil is running the show, he'll take you farther than you wanted to go and keep you there longer than you planned to stay.

God knows all these things about sin, about our seeking pleasure outside of His will for us. And He has a plan for us to enjoy pleasure and good feelings.

IT'S ALL GOOD

Have you ever watched one of those cooking shows or commercials on television that talks about the most scrumptious chocolate desserts using words such as *sinful* or *decadent*? That's an example of how a lot of us tend to view pleasure. Somehow, we believe that if something feels good, then it must be sinful.

This may come as a surprise to you, but God isn't against pleasure. In fact, the Bible is very clear that God loves pleasure. He loves to enjoy Himself, and He wants us to enjoy ourselves, too.

We're all familiar with the creation story in the first chapter of Genesis. God constructed the entire cosmos—all the planets, stars, galaxies, and other celestial bodies—then created and perfected the earth. He spoke light into existence, made night and day, and created all the plants and animals that would live here. Then God crowned His creation with the very beings He made the earth for in the first place—us!

Over and over in the creation story, we see the words "God saw that it was good." But it gets even better than good. When God had finished creating everything, including humankind, He sat back and looked at all He had made and saw that "it was *very* good" (Genesis 1:31).

You may never have thought of it this way, but the creation story is one of God thoroughly enjoying Himself. From eternity past, God has enjoyed being God, so much so that He wanted to create beings with whom He could share Himself so that they could enjoy Him, too.

Jesus once said to His disciples, "Fear not, little flock, for it is your Father's good *pleasure* to give you the kingdom" (Luke 12:32, italics mine). God really doesn't change, does He? This is a picture of a God who not only loves us, but who takes pleasure in us and who actually enjoys the idea of giving us Himself and His kingdom.

A lot of people today believe they have two choices: be spiritual or have fun. They believe that serving God means giving up all pleasures; if they choose the way of sin and the devil, at least they'll have a good time in this life. Sadly, a lot of Christians buy into that line of thinking. While they may not say or think it in those very words, they have somehow gotten the idea that being a Christian means giving up all pleasure.

But we need to understand that our choice isn't between pleasure and God. Taking that a step further, I'd say that choosing God means choosing pleasure—*eternal* pleasure.

Our Ultimate, Eternal Pleasure

When we get to heaven, we'll live in the uninterrupted knowledge and enjoyment of God. We'll take infinite pleasure in Him and He'll take infinite pleasure in us. There will never be a moment of boredom, discouragement, depression, frustration, anguish, or pain, only the pleasure of living in the presence of the Lord forever.

That sounds like the ultimate pleasure, does it not?

But that doesn't mean we aren't to enjoy the pleasures of God in this life. In fact, God desires more than anything that we take pleasure in Him *in the here and now*. But we need to realize that God will share with us His pleasure only on His terms. What's more, God wants us to take pleasure first in Him.

King David caught hold of this truth. He wrote about the pleasure of knowing God:

You make known to me the path of life;
in your presence there is fullness of joy;
at your right hand are pleasures forevermore.

PSALM 16:11

That's a lesson that the life of Moses teaches us. The New Testament tells us this about him:

By faith Moses, when he was grown up, refused to be called the son of Pharaoh's daughter, choosing rather to be mistreated with the people of God than to enjoy the fleeting pleasures of sin. He considered the reproach of Christ greater wealth than the treasures of Egypt, for he was looking to the reward.

HEBREWS 11:24–26

Moses knew more than a little about the pleasures of this world. He grew up in the home of Pharaoh and had all the money, power, and prestige a son of Egypt's leader would have. He really was living the uptown life.

But God put Moses in a place where he had to make a decision. He had all the pleasure of the world any man could want, but one day he had to face the all-important question we all must face: Which is more important and worth following—the pleasures of this world or the pleasures of God?

Moses found out that seeking the pleasures of God instead of the pleasures of the world meant inconvenience, problems, and difficulties. He found out that it meant giving up temporal pleasures for eternal ones. But he also found out that there was great reward in seeking the pleasures of God.

Moses didn't choose the pleasures of God over the pleasures of the world simply because he was a spiritual man or because he loved God. Yes, both of those things were true about Moses, but there was also a practical, benefit-oriented side to his decision. Hebrews 11:26 says that Moses "was looking to the reward."

Moses knew that if he chose the pleasures of the world, he'd have fame, power, wealth, and all the pleasures he could stand. He knew that it would "feel good" to stay right where he was. But he also knew that following the will of God and seeking pleasure in Him first meant a reward that would last for all of eternity.

Had Moses chosen the temporary pleasures of Egypt, it's likely that few of us would know who he was. But because he chose to pursue the pleasures of God, his name is now great in the Hall of Faith. Moses ended up being highly regarded by God and held in high esteem on earth to this very day. And on top of that, Moses was rewarded with everlasting rewards, reserved for those who make God their first pleasure.

We all have the same kind of decision that Adam and Eve and Moses had to make. Will we choose the illusion of the seasonal pleasures this world offers? Or will we choose to take pleasure in God first, ensuring ourselves the kind of eternal reward Moses is enjoying at this very moment?

SOME FINAL WORDS

We've all heard the old saying, "The more things change, the more they stay the same." That's certainly true of the devil.

From the time of Creation, Satan has had an ultimate goal in mind for each of us, and that is the destruction of our souls. And if he can't accomplish that—and for those of us who know Jesus Christ as our Lord and Savior, he can't—then he's satisfied with making sure that we're weak, ineffectual Christians capable of doing little or nothing to influence the world around us for God's kingdom.

To that end, the devil uses his weapons of choice against us: lies, despicable lies, and damnable lies! Every one of Satan's lies is designed to do one thing: deceive us by contradicting the truth of the Word of God. The devil's lies can be summed up in one big lie, the whopper of all eternity: We can't believe God or His written Word, the Bible. In other words, Satan tells us, God is a liar!

The devil is the most accomplished liar there ever was. He's crafty and intelligent beyond anything we mere humans can comprehend, and he knows what kind of lies each of us will fall for. However, there's something we need to understand about how God sees Satan's ability to lie and deceive.

He's not impressed.

You see, the Lord has one big advantage when it comes to countering the lies of the devil, and it's this: His character, nature, and personality. The Bible is filled from cover to cover—from the first verse in Genesis to the last in Revelation—with promise after promise from the mouth of God Himself. And not one of those promises has He failed to keep in the past or will He fail to keep in the future.

We can always count on God to do as He says He will do. As the writer of the letter to the Hebrews put it: "For when God made a promise to Abraham, since he had no one greater by whom to swear, he swore by himself, saying, 'Surely I will bless you and multiply you'" (Hebrews 6:13–14).

There is no higher character or higher word of authority than those of our God. For that reason, He need swear by no one's name but His own. And despite all the lies the devil may tell about our God, we can trust Him to back up everything He's said and every promise He's made.

For now, the devil is having a field day on planet earth, spreading his lies and wreaking havoc on all of humankind. But that isn't going to last forever. Our God *will* prevail over the devil, and He'll prevail because His Word is truth—absolute, ironclad, you-can-bank-on-it, eternal truth.

The only question each of us has to answer is, Whose words am I going to believe? Those of a spiritual enemy who hates us more than we can imagine, or those of a heavenly Father whose love for us surpasses our ability to comprehend?

See these other titles from Tony Evans

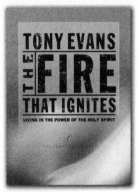

The Fire That Ignites
1-59052-083-1

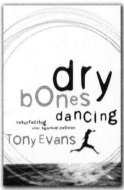

Dry Bones Dancing
1-59052-391-1

God Is More Than Enough
1-59052-337-7

TONY EVANS

**Senior Pastor of Oak Cliff Bible
Fellowship, Dallas, TX**

BIG CHANGE

**For a complete list of Big Change
titles, visit our website at
www.bigchangemoments.com**

SMALL BOOKS
BIG CHANGE®